PARIS TRAVEL JOURNAL

THIS BOOK BELONGS TO

_____

PARIS TRAVEL JOURNAL

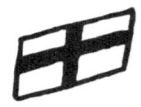

Hi there! Hope you're ready to enjoy your Paris tour with us. Before you go, we've got a few checklists to make sure you've got everything you need.

This Paris Travel Journal will be great to jot down few memories during your trip so you can look back and remember all the fun things you did. You can also share it with your friends and family when you return!

This is your official journal to write down what you see, hear, smell and taste while you are in Paris!

What was your favorite tour, food, experience?
What did you see that you weren't expecting?
Who did you meet?

FIRST A LITTLE PREPARATION FOR THE TRIP!

WHAT WILL I PACK ON THIS TRIP TO PARIS

Packing checklist!

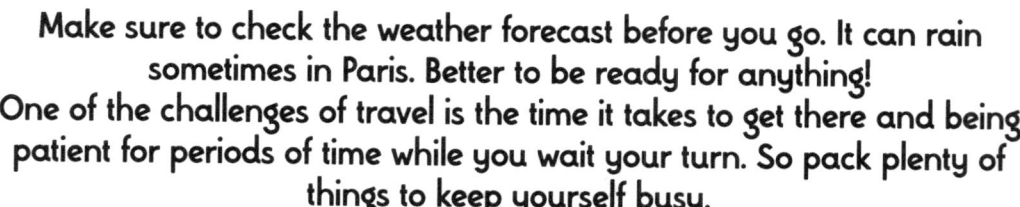

Make sure to check the weather forecast before you go. It can rain sometimes in Paris. Better to be ready for anything!
One of the challenges of travel is the time it takes to get there and being patient for periods of time while you wait your turn. So pack plenty of things to keep yourself busy.

ITEMs	How Many?	ITEMs	How Many?
Pants		Download movies	
Shorts (or skirts!)		Backpack	
Shirts		· Tablet	
Jacket or sweatshirts		· This travel journal!	
Raincoat with hood or a hat		· Andrew & Ashley's European Tours Paris Guidebook & Journal ☺	
Hat to shade from sun			
Sunglasses			
Walking shoes (tennies)		· Andrew & Ashley's European Tours Olympic Journal	
Nicer shoes for going out to a play or dinner			
Socks		· Pen, pencil, coloring pens	
Underwear!		· Book to read	
Pajamas		· Headphones	
Toothbrush		· Passport and IDs	

Check with an adult who is going on the trip with you for other things you might need and put them on your list above!

WHAT I NEED TO GET AROUND PARIS.

Pre-travel Checklist

An adult in your group should have this information at the ready either on their cell phone or printed out:

___ App or website with a map of the underground Metro

___ A taxi app on their phone

___ Tickets for reserved tours with QR codes for everyone

___ Itinerary or tour plan by day with location addresses and mode of transportation plan

___ GPS app on someone's mobile phone

___ Name and address of the hotel where you're staying

___ Cell and data roaming on your smart phones for France

TRAVEL TIPS

Many museums now have an app with an audio guide that you can load onto your cell phone. Or you can rent an audio guide at the museum. Check with your adults on how you want to handle that.

Remember, it's important to be organized to make sure you don't miss a thing! The travel time between places might be longer than you think.

Got everything organized?
You're READY! Let's go travel!

TO JOG YOUR MEMORY – HERE'S A MAP OF WHERE WE'RE GOING

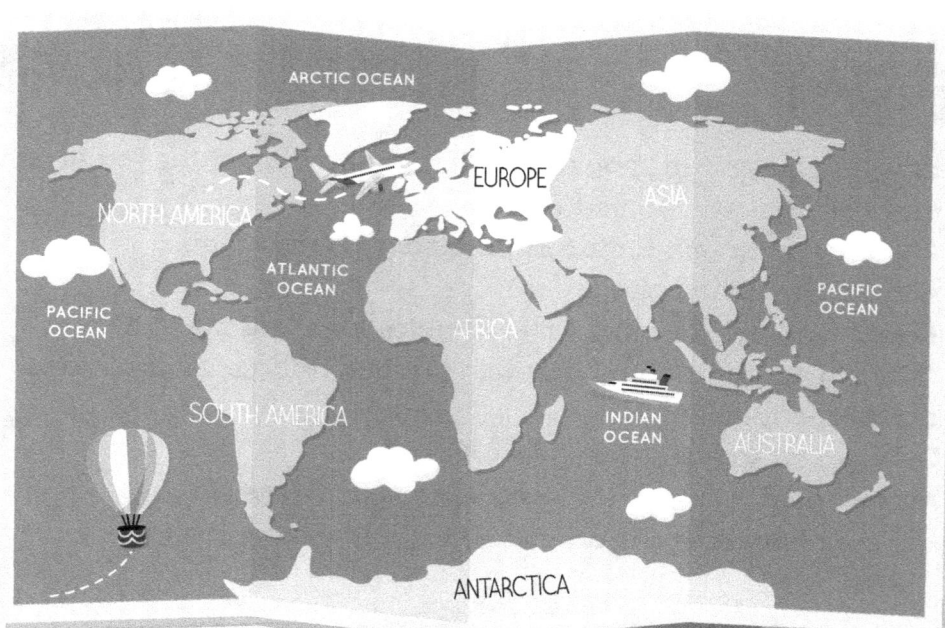

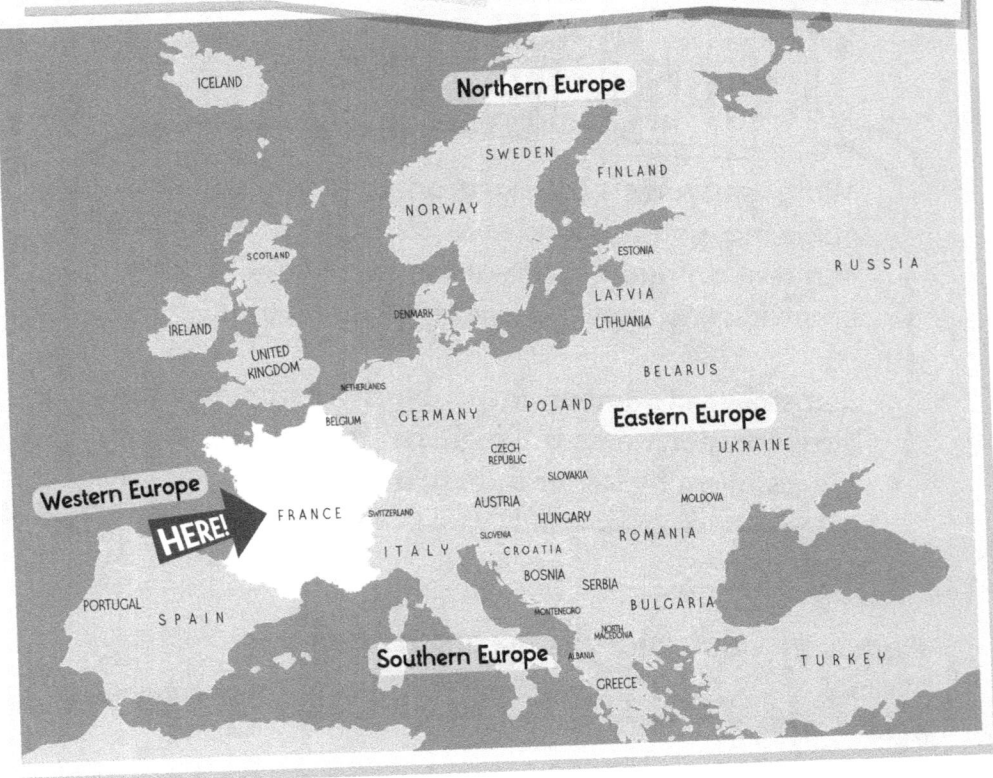

WHERE ARE YOU COMING FROM, AND HOW ARE YOU GETTING TO PARIS

My home is here:

City or Town _____

State _____

Country _____

This is how I will get to Paris:

__ Airplane

__ Car

__ Train

__ Bus

__ Other: _____

We traveled from this city before getting to Paris:

_____

If you are flying, what type of airplane is it?
(Hint: you can find out in the seat front pocket guide.)

_____

Paris has several airports, at which one will you land?

__ Charles de Gaulle

__ Orly

__ Other: _____

How will I get to Paris from the airport?

__ Taxi

__ The Underground

__ App Taxi

__ Tour Bus

__ Train

__ Other: _____

What hotel are you staying at, in Paris?

_____

PARIS
TRAVEL JOURNAL

While you travel, you're going to want to write down some of the great things you've seen, heard and tasted.

Use this guide on your trip and after you return to create a record of everything. It's so nice to look back on it later!

I'm betting your friends and family will love to hear about it too.

PARIS **FOOD** CULTURE:

When you visit other countries, there will always be unique food to try. The important thing is that you try it so you know whether you want to eat it again. When you're an adult you may come back.

What was your favorite food you tried in Paris, or how about your least favorite?

Favorite food I tasted in Paris:

_____

Least favorite food I tasted in Paris:

_____

Did you eat in a bistro? What was that like?

_____

Food I tasted while in Paris

___ Croque-Monsieur
___ Croque-Madame
___ Croissant
___ Omelette
___ Quiche
___ Eclair
___ Charcuteire
___ Sandwich Jambon Beurre
___ French cheese
___ French chocolate

PARIS ART CULTURE:

We hope you had time to visit the museums where so much famous art and artifacts are on display.

What was your favorite artist and painting you saw in Paris?

Favorite painting I saw in Paris:

_____

What was the artists name?

_____

Other types of art I saw:

_____

PARIS THEATRE CULTURE:

As we've mentioned, the plays and musicals in Paris are some of the best in the world. Did you go see a play or musical?

Even if you didn't get the time, what do you want to see?

A play or musical I saw while in Paris:

_____

A play or musical I wanted to see while in Paris:

_____

If you were lucky enough to go to the theatre, glue or tape your ticket or a cut out from the brochure below:

PARIS MUSIC CULTURE:

Music is all around us in the world, but you may or may not have had time to go to a live music event or learn about musicians.

Did you see any musicians in the streets or in restaurants?

My favorite music by a Parisian artist is:

_____

My least favorite is:

_____

If you took a photo walking on the road or in front of the studio, glue or tape your photo here!

PARIS BOOKS & MOVIES CULTURE:

In Andrew & Ashley's Paris travel guide we listed many books that turned into movies. So much to see on this subject.

What is your favorite French book that is also a movie?

Favorite French book that is also a movie:

_____

A French book or movie I liked when I was younger, but I've moved on: 😊

_____

Draw your favorite character here, or glue or tape a picture of them:

PARIS SPORTS CULTURE:

Did you know that Paris had so many sporting events for people to attend? Did you get a chance to go to one? The football (soccer) events get quite loud. If you got a chance to go to a game, how did the noise and all the fans cheering make you feel?

I saw a group of people wearing their team's jerseys, which teams were they?

_____

I went to a sporting event, and here's what I liked about it:

_____

My favorite professional or social sport in France is:

_____

Draw or trace your favorite sport from the book here:

PARIS FAMOUS PEOPLE CULTURE:

We hope you got a chance to learn about the famous people in France. Which one is your favorite?

My favorite French famous person:

_____

What does this person do that you like the most:

_____

When you visited all the monumets. What kind of jobs did you see people doing?

_____

Draw or trace your favorite royal famous person
from the book here:

DID YOU TRY SPEAKING A LITTLE FRENCH?

Where were you when you heard someone speaking French?

Did it make you giggle? You can even turn on the television to hear them!

Places I heard different accents in Paris:

_____

_____

_____

What is your favorite word in French?

_____

Did you go to a boulongerie during your visit?

Did you say "bonjour" while you were visiting?

Did you see any mimes?

What's the French word for thank you? _____

What's the French word for your favorite pastry? _____

PEOPLE I MET OR SAW WHILE I WAS IN PARIS

We try to strike up conversations with the people we meet when we travel. It makes it more fun and sometimes we find out about cool stuff going on.

Did you ask any questions or strike up a conversation with people you met? Did you meet any kids your age?

Hotel workers

Restaurant workers

Tour guides

Pilot or airline workers

Store clerks

Football fans

People in a pub

People at dinner or lunch

Museum workers

Theatre workers

Other

Other kids

Famous people

Actors

Sports people

Models

Other _____

Darn! I wish I would have seen someone famous, but I had fun anyway.

MY FAVORITE THINGS I LIKED ABOUT PARIS

During the whole trip, the things I liked the most was:
- the culture
- the tours
- all the forms of transportation
- the people I met
- all the accents I heard
- the museums
- the theatre
- the monuments and statues
- stories about artists and their subjects
- chateaus
- learning about sports!
- other

Write about your experiences here:

Andrew and Ashley gave you a list of their top places to visit while in Paris. Let's start with this list — did you have any favorites here?

Eiffel Tower	Catacombs
Arc de Triomphe	Arènes de Lutèce
Champs-Élysées	Moulin Rouge
Luxor Obelisk	Tuileries Gardens
Aquarium	Latin Quarter
River Seine boat ride	West Bank
Notre Dame Cathedral	St. Germain Boulevard
Sacre Coeur	Pantheon
ChocoStory tour	Jardin du Luxembourg
Palace of Versaille	Flyview
Disneyland	Shakespeare Book Shop
The Louvre Museum	

Pick YOUR TOP 5 tours and list them on the next page!

COLOR IN PARIS

A famous Paris icon in this picture.
What is it?_____

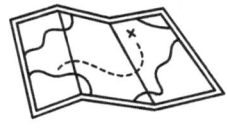

MY PARIS TRIP JOURNAL

What were my TOP 5 favorite places to visit?

FAVORITE PLACES

Visit #1: _____

Visit #2: _____

Visit #3: _____

Visit #4: _____

Visit #5: _____

Later in the book you can write in a journal page about it.
First let's find out what you liked about Paris in general!

My #1 favorite visit was:

_____

It was my #1 favorite because:

_____

My favorite thing I saw was:

_____

Something I saw that I've never seen before:

_____

Who was the most famous person mentioned on this tour:

_____

The part I didn't like was:

_____

Something I'm going to tell people about when I get home is:

_____

Something I found weird or funny (and maybe kinda wonderful) about this visit:

_____

Draw, glue or tape something from your tour here:

Overall rating for this or event tour is: _____ stars

Color in the number of stars above to indicate your score!

On this tour or at this event I learned about:

- people's lives
- art
- royalty
- people's jobs
- famous people
- history
- culture
- government
- sports
- other

On this tour or at this event I heard:

- funny words
- horses
- sports fans getting excited
- music
- loud noises
- traffic sounds
- people laughing
- a tour guide talking
- an audience clapping
- other

Write in your journal in your own words what you experienced, who you met, what you liked, or didn't!

_____

_____

_____

_____

_____

_____

_____

My #2 favorite visit was:

_____

It was my #2 favorite because:

_____

My favorite thing I saw was:

_____

Something I saw that I've never seen before:

_____

Who was the most famous person mentioned on this tour:

_____

The part I didn't like was:

_____

Something I'm going to tell people about when I get home is:

_____

Something I found weird or funny (and maybe kinda wonderful) about this visit:

_____

Draw, glue or tape something from your tour here:

Overall rating for this or event tour is: _____ stars

Color in the number of stars above to indicate your score!

On this tour or at this event I learned about:

- people's lives
- art
- royalty
- people's jobs
- famous people
- history
- culture
- government
- sports
- other

On this tour or at this event I heard:

- funny words
- horses
- sports fans getting excited
- music
- loud noises
- traffic sounds
- people laughing
- a tour guide talking
- an audience clapping
- other

Write in your journal in your own words what you experienced, and who you met, what you liked, or didn't!

_____

_____

_____

_____

_____

_____

_____

My #3 favorite visit was:

_____

It was my #3 favorite because:

_____

My favorite thing I saw was:

_____

Something I saw that I've never seen before:

_____

Who was the most famous person mentioned on this tour:

_____

The part I didn't like was:

_____

Something I'm going to tell people about when I get home is:

_____

Something I found weird or funny (and maybe kinda wonderful) about this visit:

_____

Draw, glue or tape something from your tour here:

Overall rating for this or event tour is: ____ stars

Color in the number of stars above to indicate your score!

On this tour or at this event I learned about:

- people's lives
- art
- royalty
- people's jobs
- famous people
- history
- culture
- government
- sports
- other

On this tour or at this event I heard:

- funny words
- horses
- sports fans getting excited
- music
- loud noises
- traffic sounds
- people laughing
- a tour guide talking
- an audience clapping
- other

Write in your journal in your own words what you experienced, and who you met, what you liked, or didn't!

_____

_____

_____

_____

_____

_____

_____

My #4 favorite visit was:

_____

It was my #4 favorite because:

_____

My favorite thing I saw was:

_____

Something I saw that I've never seen before:

_____

Who was the most famous person mentioned on this tour:

_____

The part I didn't like was:

_____

Something I'm going to tell people about when I get home is:

_____

Something I found weird or funny (and maybe kinda wonderful) about this visit:

_____

Draw, glue or tape something from your tour here:

Overall rating for this or event tour is: _____ stars

Color in the number of stars above to indicate your score!

On this tour or at this event I learned about:

- people's lives
- art
- royalty
- people's jobs
- famous people
- history
- culture
- government
- sports
- other

On this tour or at this event I heard:

- funny words
- horses
- sports fans getting excited
- music
- loud noises
- traffic sounds
- people laughing
- a tour guide talking
- an audience clapping
- other

Write in your journal in your own words what you experienced, and who you met, what you liked, or didn't!

_____

_____

_____

_____

_____

_____

_____

My #5 favorite visit was:

_____

It was my #5 favorite because:

_____

My favorite thing I saw was:

_____

Something I saw that I've never seen before:

_____

Who was the most famous person mentioned on this tour:

_____

The part I didn't like was:

_____

Something I'm going to tell people about when I get home is:

_____

Something I found weird or funny (and maybe kinda wonderful) about this visit:

_____

Draw, glue or tape something from your tour here:

Overall rating for this or event tour is: _____ stars

Color in the number of stars above to indicate your score!

On this tour or at this event I learned about:

- people's lives
- art
- royalty
- people's jobs
- famous people
- history
- culture
- government
- sports
- other

On this tour or at this event I heard:

- funny words
- horses
- sports fans getting excited
- music
- loud noises
- traffic sounds
- people laughing
- a tour guide talking
- an audience clapping
- other

Write in your journal in your own words what you experienced, and who you met, what you liked, or didn't!

_____

_____

_____

_____

_____

_____

_____

COLOR IN PARIS

Name the historical place in this picture? _____

JOURNAL PAGES

Write down, draw, or paste something about your trip!
Consider adding a date and what you saw, who you met,
and what you learned.

JOURNAL PAGES

Write down, draw, or paste something about your trip!
Consider adding a date and what you saw, who you met,
and what you learned.

JOURNAL PAGES

Write down, draw, or paste something about your trip!
Consider adding a date and what you saw, who you met,
and what you learned.

Andrew & Ashley's EUROPEAN TOURS

www.ingramcontent.com/pod-product-compliance
Lightning Source LLC
Chambersburg PA
CBHW082113120626
46553CB00011B/3668